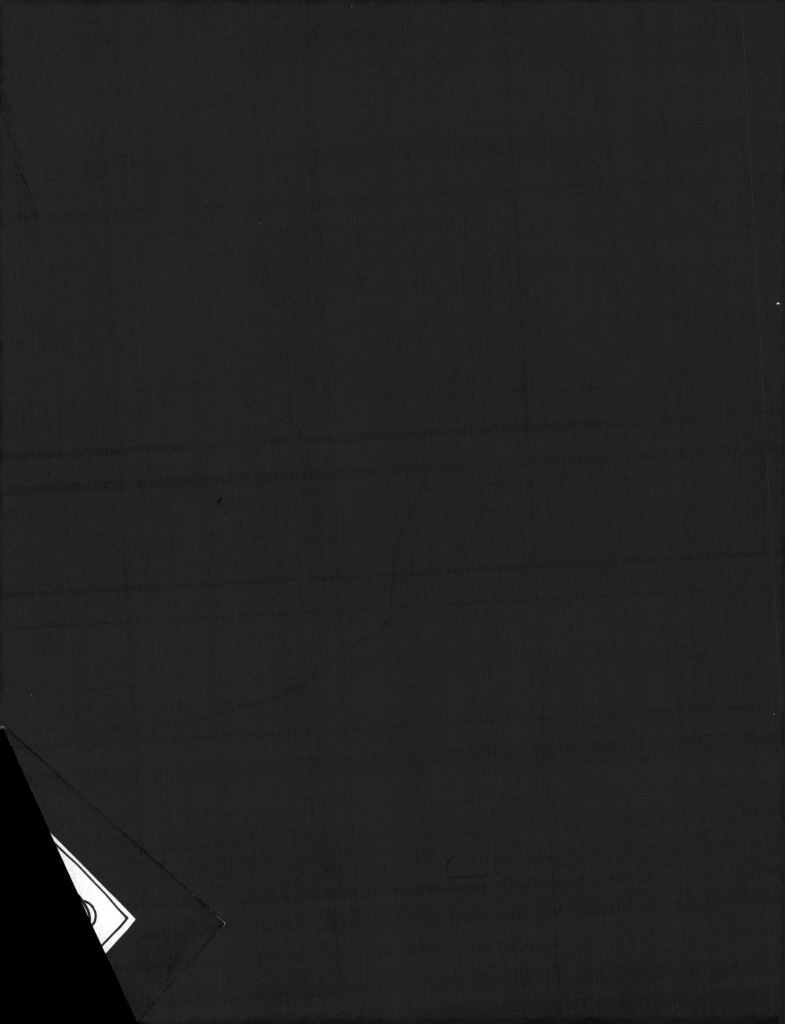

Turn stress into success!

A motivational and inspirational adult
coloring book.

Color your stress away, take control of your
life, and do a little bit of ass-kicking.

THAT'S ALL.

Check out **SwearWordColoringBook.com** for free adult coloring pages and info on all of my books.

Don't forget to sign up to my **email list** and receive **free goodies** from time to time!

Happy fucking coloring.

DO MORE

of what makes

YOU

FUCKING

HAPPY.

WAKE UP.

Kick Ass.

REPEAT.

Fuck! Nothing left to color.

But, if you want more to color,
buy one of these other titles
from John T!

Made in the USA
Lexington, KY
17 June 2017